# ROYAL CONVERSATIONS

## How to Develop a Lifestyle of Diplomacy

*By*

## Prof. Julian Businge

## and

## HRH King Okogyeman Kobina Amissah 1

## (Sir Clyde Rivers)

Greatness University Publishers
London, UK
www.greatnessuniversity.co.uk

**ISBN: 978-1-913164-27-0**
**ISBN-13: 978-1-913164-27-0**

# How to Develop a Lifestyle of Diplomacy

## DISCLAIMER

This publication and the accompanying materials are designed to provide accurate and authoritative information in regard to the subject matter covered in it. It is provided with the understanding that the publisher is not engaged in rendering legal, accounting, or other professional opinions. If legal advice or other expert assistance is required, the services of a competent professional should be sought.

## DEDICATION

This work is devoted to each person who is on a path of developing a lifestyle of royal diplomacy; and seeks greater understanding on the kingdom of God. Now is the right time for the royal giant inside you to arise and crush the inner critic. Identity crisis is the lack of knowledge about who we truly are. Give yourself the gift of knowing and embracing your royal identity. May you enjoy royalty at its best!

# CONTENTS

# ACKNOWLEDGMENTS

God bless you all who have made this publication possible and may His Kingdom come through you.

# PREFACE

We are living so far below the mind of GOD. It is possible to operate and function with the thought patterns of GOD.

A Lifestyle of Diplomacy means that Believers have greater authority in the Spiritual realm through Christ Jesus. Unrealized, we become destructive rather than constructive and end up destroying the people we are supposed to preserve like an atheists who can became a Christian by seeing God's supernatural power show up among everyday people.

The Holy Spirit continues to move supernaturally, drawing people to Jesus with signs, wonders and miracles. God calls each of us to a lifestyle of diplomacy. He desires for us to live out Jesus' promise that we would do even "greater works" than what He did (John 14:12).

When God sees your mountain, He says "Speak to the mountain and the mountain shall be removed."
If you are going to grab the perspective of God, you have got to look at that mountain from a different perspective. Look at it from God's perspective.

What you see is all that He can see because He made you in His image. If you don't see far, He doesn't see far.

If you receive evil thoughts, you paint evil doings in your life. If you receive God's thoughts, you do God's thoughts in your life.

Every person that has ever achieved in life talked about it before they walked about it.
We have been walking in principles of faith without even knowing it. Walkout those principles right now! Words have created that very mountain in your life. Words will bring it down.

Understand that power is in the words in your mouth. Don't get stuck in a negative mindset. Turn the corner.

You do good, good comes back to you. You do bad, bad comes back to you. It's a law of karma. When you speak life with your mouth you set a law in motion. This is the time to develop a mindset that you're made in the image of God and therefore, you must turn your conceptualities to reality.

You were born to dominate and not to be dominated. We are sons and daughters of the heavenly kind! We are no more slaves to fear! Every doubt must be conquered!

# INTRODUCTION

In this book, 'Royal Conversations - How to Develop a Lifestyle of Diplomacy', we are going to learn a skill that absolutely will unlock our leadership potential. We've learned in one way or the other to do things differently, to rethink responses to the disruptive forces that change our society. In fact, some of us are fired up to run out ahead of the accelerating pace of change today. We need to slow down and pay attention to the disappearing art of diplomacy. You will agree with me that, diplomacy is brutally time consuming, but if you can develop it, you won't regret. This is the main reason you need to read this book. It will be worth every second.

Are you a CEO, father, mother or a member of a Non-Governmental Organization (NGO)? Then you're a diplomat and therefore you need to do things like a diplomat. Developing a life of diplomacy will be your key to doing things the right way and leading those under you. We'll be far more effective promoting change if we're a diplomat.

But we will be profitable if we allow God to be all in all for us. We've got to believe. Let's read Mark 9: 23-24: Jesus said unto him, "If you can believe, all things are possible to him who believes.
 24: Immediately the father of the child cried out and said with tears, "Lord, I believe: help my unbelief!"

As a child of God, it's time you change your mindset, and renew your thoughts and ways of thinking. Our heavenly Father never intended for us to live according to the world's system and ways of thinking, behaving, and overall ways of doing things. God admonished us in Hebrews 10:38 to live by FAITH. He said, "Now the just shall live by faith; but if anyone draws back, my soul has no pleasure in him." Without faith, it's impossible to please God. Our God wants those who call on Him to believe in Him, and trust that He rewards those who diligently seek after Him (Hebrews 11:6).

*This book, Royal Conversations is designed to help the reader* understand that there's power in the words of your mouth and that you can command God's blessings on your life. This book will help you not to get stuck in a negative mindset.

God is looking for people of faith. If you can develop your mindset and thoughts toward the things of God, you can change the way you view and do things—eating, giving, working out, and building relationships.

Do you know changing your mindset can change your circumstances? Your mind is powerful. It has the power to bring life or to bring destruction, as everything starts with a thought. How you think determines how you live. In this book, we provide examples of people who changed their mindset and by God's grace, it was well with them. From today, you also can be assured it will be well with you!

All you need to do is:

- Be strong and courageous
- Do not turn from the Bible to the left or right
- Be careful to obey the Bible
- Do not let the Book of the Law depart from your mouth
- Mediate on the Word of God day and night.

You want God to take away all the suffering, sickness, problems, pain, and sadness. But God wants to work on you first, because transformation won't happen in your life until you renew your mind or until your thoughts begin to change. Hence, why it is so important that you learn how to manage your mind. Your thoughts control your *LIFE.*

Your thoughts have tremendous ability to shape your life for good or for bad. With Royal Conversations & How to Develop a Lifestyle of Diplomacy, things change for the better. We focus so much on changing our mindset, because the mind is the battleground for sin.

The God who led His people through the parted sea and from Egyptian bondage; who rained down bread from heaven all the pilgrim way is the God to whom we pray.

The God who rescued Daniel from the lion's den; saved the three young men from the fiery furnace; who speaks and constellations will His voice obey, is the same God to whom we pray.

The God who stills the tempest with a word divine, and on the clouds of sorrow, makes His rainbows shine, who from the tomb of Jesus rolled the stone away, is the God whom we pray

The God who clothes the lily in its robe of snow, who in the barren desert makes His rivers flow, the God who lifts the sinner from the miry clay, is the God whom we pray.

# ROYAL PRIESTHOOD IN CHRIST

Royal Ambassadorship and Royal Diplomacy means that we can increase in understanding not only our identity but what is necessary to fulfil our destiny in God. Surely as God has redeemed us, he also esteemed us as Kings and Priests and we will find that in Revelations 5:9-10. It is something that over the years I have noticed that not much emphasis is placed on our identity in Christ.

He not only redeemed us, the Bible says He redeemed us to God and has made us kings and priests so as surely as we believe we are redeemed as surely he has esteemed us. So we are redeemed and we are esteemed and that is the proper balance that I bring to the teachings that God has given to me. And that truth has to permeate everything that you do, so as royalty not only is that our identity to walk with God, it is also what is necessary to get us to fulfil our destiny because it's our legal identity in Christ and He is the King of kings –who are the kings that he is king of. Well he is our king so that understating is what brings us to the rule as Priests and our rule as Kings. So we have a role and responsibility as priests to minister and then we have the rule as Kings.

When God created us in Genesis, he said "Go yield" so there was a field, go dominate and be fruitful. For you to be fruitful there must be a field for you to do so many things. To exercise your gifts, we are co-creating with God everything we see around us we just work hand in hand, it's so amazing

we are sharing in the ruler ship and we are sharing in the representation of Christ. So when He redeemed us to God and made us Kings and Priests, He said now you get to share in my royalty. Royalty is conferred to us and it's not something that we have earned, lest should we boast or brag.

We are royal by blood so that's the first thing we share in the royalty of Christ, we share in the ruler ship of Christ and we share in the representation of Christ and that in itself is a high calling. Royalty is a high calling. So our devoted pursuit as citizens of the Kingdom of God, as members of his royal priesthood it should be our devoted pursuit to walk worthy of the calling with which we are called.

So not only are we called to share, it's a high calling and without training without consummate skill, without grooming, we will not be able to walk worthy of that calling and this is why training is necessary. There is no person, viable partaker of any royal monarchy or establishment that enters without preparation.

Even in the natural, they are groomed, they are prepared, they are trained and so this is why I believe specialized training is necessary so that with the high calling we can walk worthy. According to Ephesians 4:1, it says" walk worthy of the calling with which you are called". Let's walk worthy, be trained, develop and cultivate the skills that are needed to get us into that high calling because we are running around saying am royalty, am King's daughter, am this and that but are you walking worthy in your royalty, are you walking worthy in your ruler ship, in your representation of the King.

## The Royal Generosity

Giving is so important to God, not only does he give but he gives exceedingly, abundantly above all. Much as He gives, He requires us to do the same. You cannot go to God without a gift, you can never come in the presence of God empty handed because if in His goodness He can load you every morning, how dare you come back to him empty handed. So in our physical world as well when we are meeting each other as royals we have to display the same thing.

1 Kings: 10, when the Queen of Sheba came to Solomon the Bible tells u and I quote this because I believe in this so much. It says "Now King Solomon gave the Queen of Sheba all she desired, whatever she asked besides what Solomon had given her according to Royal generosity".

He gave the Queen of Sheba according to the royal generosity, so it's written. Then we read in Esther where the King gave gifts according to the generosity of a king. One of the ways you can distinguish a king is their ability to be generous. They are generous with their time, generous with their help, their finances.

According to the word of God, one of the ways we can identify a king is by their royal generosity. A true king is not cheap, they give gifts according to the generosity of a king and that comes from their generous heart because think of it; the God or the King we serve or that we emanate from because we are ambassadors of Christ for Christ is generous with us, he does not deprive us of anything that is beneficial for us, he daily loads us with benefits, that's generosity.

He supplies us with whatever we need, all we have ever needed His hand provides, He is a generous King and if we are representing a generous King then in accordance with His generosity we also must be generous. Now it doesn't mean that we do it ill-advised or unadvised but I believe that the spirit of God in us has to be representative of the king that we said we serve.

Generosity is one of the principles for every Royal. , it distinguishes a King, one who is called to walk in this royalty You shall know them by their fruits. So if they say they are royals, how are they bringing the kingdom of God into existence, how are they walking worthy of that calling, how are they manifesting.

The world is awaiting our ascension, our manifestation, our demonstration, our elevation so that when we are elevated because we cannot take persons where we have not been so it's time that we begin to demonstrate or cultivate the characteristics that are consistent with who we are. If we say we are royalty then our behavior, our mannerisms, our characteristics should be consistent with who we say we are.

# The Royal Conduct and Behavior

How do you carry yourself, are you an exemplary example in your workplace, in your marriage, in your parenting, ministry anywhere God places or positions you? 1Samuel 10:25 and it says that "Samuel explained to the people the behavior of Royalty" there was a certain department of royalty, there is a certain way that royalty carries itself. It's not an arrogant behavior, its confidence in who God has called you to be.

When a king is faced with great trials, encountering situations, Kings behave in a manner that is consistent with who they are. Royal behavior cannot be overlooked, cannot be under estimated. You never hear of a King speaking luck, wondering how he is going to pay his bills, you never hear our king cursing out other people.

So then how is it that we will easily say am a daughter of the king, child of the king -that is true. We cannot refute or debate that but what we can debate is the fruit that you exhibit that is inconsistent with what you say you are and whose you are.

The issue here is not in our abilities per say but in our mentalities. Do we mentally agree with God, do we have the mind of Christ when it comes to understanding who he has made us to be and that is where if it's not in our spirit and flowing from our heart then there will be inconsistencies all the time.

But when I know whose I am and who I am in God that affects the way and influences every decision that I make. I am not going to be worried as a daughter of the King, the Bible tells me "the birds of the air toil not, neither do they speak yet your heavenly father looks after them, then he says are you not of more value than them.

So if the birds don't worry where they getting their next meal from, how then as a king am I concerned to the point of worrying how I will be fed. The Bible says "seek first the Kingdom of God and his righteousness and all these things shall be added unto you" so when I think like that am thinking in a manner consistent with what the word of God by constitution.

The word of God is the constitution of the kingdom. My constitution constitutes how I live, how I think, how I behave. So in accordance with the constitution, the constitution tells me don't worry, so as a King I have to elevate my thoughts that I am not going to ascend into worry, am going to ascend into worship.

One of the ways of conducting yourself in royalty, one of them would be meekness. The Bible says "God resists the proud, but that gives grace to the humble". Even though we know we are royalty God has given us power we have the king, we are dawned with so much power, we carry so much grace and angels are watching over us, we must walk in humility.

The Bible says "if any man thinks of himself to be something and he is nothing, he deceives himself" in the book of Revelations. Well we are not deceiving ourselves we are royals by blood, by the blood of Christ.

He redeemed us and He esteemed us to share in His royalty and I can't think of any other blessing that gives me grace and peace and excitement to know that in this lifetime someone thought me worthy enough to become royalty. It's such a honor and it's a honor of royalty.

So where we understand that this is conferred on us the Bible says "it's not by works lest any man should boast" so the only boast thing we do is our boast is in the lord. We brag on our father being a King and he has given us access to share in his Kingship and that is amazing.

This truly is Having that opportunity to reign with the King of Kings, who holds Heaven and Earth in all His sovereignty, he has given us so much power and some people don't know how much power they have. Whatsoever is bound on earth is bound in heaven, he has given us the keys to unlock, to speak, to co-create, make it happen, rule with him.

People are destroyed for a lack of knowledge, we are not living consistently or to the standard so we are looking at the standard and royalty in title doesn't mean anything if we are not functioning as royalty in standard and in stature according to his word. So if we look at Ephesians 4, here is what it says "till we all come to the unity of the faith to a perfect man to the measure of the stature of the fullness of Christ.

Training for reigning is important so the measure that God wants us to attain is fullness. We may be walking right now in a measure of our royalty but God doesn't want us to remain at the measure, he wants the measure to be the fullness in Christ.

So royalty is not just about having a title, that's not what Christ intended, He intended that we come into the fullness of Christ according to the standard and stature. In the Bible the book of Luke, we read that the child grew in wisdom and in stature and in favor with God. It is talking about Jesus, so if this is Jesus and he had to grow into this, how we proceed and think we can come into the fullness of Christ without having the goal of reigning in power.

We are pressing towards the fullness, so when we look at our lives there is something called the language of kings, the stature of kings, the generosity of kings, the royal behavior of kings, the royal priesthood, the royal robes. By king we understand that I am king because I can rule myself, we have to succeed the first level of ruler ship for us is on a personal level.

A personal dimension of ruler ship and peace must be experienced in us before we can express that dimension publicly. So if we do not succeed in governing ourselves then how can we succeed in governing the outer forces of our lives.

# The Royal Robes

*While I was discussing with Dr. Alicia M Liverpool, our dear friend, she said that she was* delighted to speak about these divine truths  because it has changed her life .when she understood this truth, she made a choice in every matter that she faced with in her lifetime on this earth." I can choose when I hear of a betrayal, when I hear of someone who wants to destroy me or when something drastic about to happen, when something painful happens.I have a choice on whose side to believe and trust, God's word is a strong tower."

Esther understood this principle; Esther 4 the word of God tells us that both Esther and Mordecai understood that Haman had a plan to kill the Jews. The Bible shows us the distinction of royalty, we can be faced in life with identical situations, identical problems and we each handle it differently why because it depends on our level of consciousness, the mind of Christ, and the royal mindset that we bring to situations.

The Bible says that Mordecai put on sackcloth and ashes and began weeping and wailing with aloud and bitter cry. The Bible says that Esther heard what was happening, she sent garments to Mordecai to change his garments but he refused. The Bible says Esther,

Chapter 5: 1, says she changed her garments and put on her royal robes and she stood in the entrance facing the king.

Mordecai put on sackcloth and ashes, Esther in the identical situation put on her royal robes and she didn't say a word. She stood before the King and got his attention, he extended the scepter to he, she drew close, and touched the scepter and she was able in a series of events to save her people.

When we are faced with difficulties, what are we putting on? sackcloth and ashes or are we putting on our royal robes. Because here is what the word of God tells us to do which is so important to realize, it says, which brings me into protocol and diplomacy, in Esther chapter 4 that "no one clothed in sackcloth and ashes may come before the King" so even though Mordecai legitimately was worried for his people, he was distressed.

The Bible says he was deeply depressed and so was Esther but even being deeply distressed, we are not free from our responsibilities. To save our world will not require us every time we see something on TV, everytime there is pandemic, an issue in the world to put on our sackcloth and ashes and be crying, weeping and wailing, we need to put on our royal garments and go before the King and plead on behalf of nations, to plead on behalf of our people.

We have been called to the kingdom for such a time as this, it is not for us to see what's happening in the world and descend in weeping and wailing with loud and bitter cries, it is time for us to pin our head up, put on our royal crown, straighten our crown, put on our royal robes and go before the king with a mandate.

Esther was able to save millions from genocide, she was able to save her people and we can do the same, we have the same power. The same God of Esther, is the same God of everyone and He does not change because He is the same yesterday, today and forever.

So if we do it according to kingdom protocols, it simply means the prescribed way, in the bible says "no one may come before the king clothed with sackcloth and ashes, so Mordecai even though he was weeping and wailing, he was violating protocol.

There was a breach in protocol and he was hoping that in violating protocol he could still come before the king, well the king was probably hearing Mordecai weeping and wailing, and the Bible says many joined Mordecai because misery loves company.

When we weep and we wail, the hurt that we are feeling is not sufficient for us to feel by ourselves we invite everybody to weep and wail with us but protocol dictates that in Psalms 100 "Come before his presence with singing, enter His gates with thanksgiving, enter His courts with praise, be thankful to Him and bless His name.

Royal Robes are very important because even in Jesus' teaching, in his parables he mentioned when he threw a feast and invited everybody to come, some people didn't go and he decided to call everybody on the street and there are some who came without preparing themselves and they were thrown out in spite of the fact that they found them on the street but you have to prepare yourself before you go to the King. you have to have an appointment, there are protocols to be followed.

## Protocol and Diplomacy

Protocol is the system of international courtesy in international relations and communications. In the Kingdom of God, protocol is the prescribed way. In the Bible, it says "as for God, His way is perfect" in Psalm 18:30. Proverbs 14 says "there is a way that seems right onto man but the end of it is the way of death".

So it seems right to us but it is not right and this is where we must confer, consult, humble ourselves and say God your way is perfect. This is why the book of proverbs tells us in all your ways acknowledge Him and he shall direct your path, what happens to us many times, we are leaning on our own understanding.

In all your ways, acknowledge Him and He will direct your path that simply means he will not lead you in a path that is inconsistent with His path, inconsistent with his will, this is why we must acknowledge him.

We must say God the way am approaching this, what is the way to approach this situation because God wants you to come out victorious and I prophesy this, God wants you to come out without injury, God doesn't want causalities in his kingdom, he doesn't want injuries in his kingdom.

You can go through a storm so we can go through situations, it doesn't mean because you are royalty that you are exempted from facing circumstances and situations, it means that you are guaranteed to come out the victorious one, to come out as the victor and not as the victim.

A few years ago HRH Clyde Rivers and Prof. Julian Businge together with other members had an opportunity to meet HRH King Oyo of Tooro Kingdom. When you are meeting him, there's a special way to greet him, you don't just say Hi, there is a protocol, you begin with praising his Royal majesty, your highness – you give them praise. So in the same manner we go to God with praise, we enter His gates with praise and thanksgiving.

Imagine you wake up one morning desiring to speak to the Queen of England. There is no way you can show up at the Buckingham Palace as a visitor or guest and say "am here to see the queen, hey queen what's up". That's not how it's done. It's by invitation into her presence.

Even another story is the prodigal son when he came back to his senses and said I will go back to my father, probably he was living with the pigs, when his father saw him he said bring him the royal robes, dress him up, they put shoes on him. All that is a meaning, he had to be dressed before entering into the house. He had to be dressed up brand new before entering into the house of his father.

We are all here on a mission, people are counting on us and He is counting on us because the Bible says "the heavens belong to God and Earth has he given unto man". So we are His children, how are we meant to function, how can we bring that kingdom of God into reality, into manifestation, into the simplest ways.

Simple things we do but we do them with knowledge and purpose, you see them as simple but when you are doing them you know the gospel demands you to do, you are bringing the kingdom of God here on earth, you are doing something incredible because when we go back to the father to the King of kings He will ask some of these thing, we will give accountability of how we spent our days and lives. We cannot hope to produce any glory on earth without Christ. Christ in you and me the hope of our glory.

# THY KINGDOM COME

Jesus teaching the Lord's prayer said when you pray, say, Our Father which art in heaven hallowed be thy name, thy kingdom come thy will be done on earth as it is in heaven. So the design of God is as it is in heaven so shall it be on earth. As my power is seen in heaven so shall be made manifest on earth. And as my influence, riches are seen all over heaven so shall it be seen on earth.

Father we ask oh God unveil yourself to us like never before, in the enforcement of the kingdom, the manifestation of the kingdom, in the name of Jesus. Jesus told us that the kingdom is not here or there but the kingdom is right within you.

In the book of Luke 16:20, the Bible says "and there was a certain beggar named Lazarus, which was laid at his gate, full of sores". Now for proper understanding verse 19 , it says "there was a certain rich man, which was clothed in purple and fine linen, and fared sumptuously every day". "and there was a certain beggar named Lazarus, which was laid at his gate, full of sores". Luke 16:21 "and desiring to be fed with crumbs which fell from the rich man's table: moreover, the dogs came and licked his sores. Luke 16:22 "and it came to pass, that the beggar died, and was carried by the angels into Abraham's bosom: the rich man also died, and was buried "and in hell he lift up his eyes, being in torments, and seeth Abraham afar off, and Lazarus in his bosom. "And he cried and said, Father Abraham, have mercy on me, and send Lazarus that he may dip the tip of his finger in water, and cool my tongue; for I am tormented in this flame." "But Abraham said, Son, remember that thou in thy lifetime received thy good things, and likewise Lazarus evil things: but now he is comforted, and thou art tormented" (KJV).

Father make your will, your word, your desire known unto kingdom on us from today. Child of God, it is interesting that we look at the man that the scripture presents to us and that is the man Lazarus and the Bible says he was at the gate of the rich man desiring to be fed from the crumbs from the rich man's table and in the course of being at the gate of the rich man that the dogs came and licked his wounds and as the dogs came, he would obviously would have died as a result of the wounds, the sores, the decay of what was going on in his body and he eventually died.

Unfortunately, the kingdom man Lazarus that made it to the other side with God did not experience the kingdom on earth and so the million-dollar question is, how can a royal eventually end up in heaven, without entering the kingdom here on earth?

Child of God, be reminded that what we are going to be manifested is not after the rapture. It's the kingdom that we are going to be insisting on even while we are here on earth and so I will not be called a kingdom child when I eventually go to heaven, I will be called a royal even as I speak, even as I walk into the office, wherever I get to and do.

The Bible says where the word of a King is, there is power, Decree and say I am a Royal, say I live in the fullness of the privileges of the kingdom while am on earth. If you believe it say a loud Amen!

But child of God, do you realize one major reason , the bible says that Lazarus, the meaning of his name Lazarus like most of us already know he is helped by God. God was involved in his life, the help of the supernatural was involved in his life but child of God, a man that God has helped is at the gate with sores, without any form of help from man, not from God Himself but see what is upsetting me about this kingdom man, my problem is not his sores, not that he is even at the gate, not even the treatment of the rich man, my major problem which God wants every child of his here to understand is his Desire.

The Bible says kingdom man Lazarus was desiring to be fed with the crumbs which fell from the rich man's table, Lazarus I don't have a problem that you are sick I have a problem with your desire. Dear Royal, the beginning of the manifestation of the kingdom is what you are thinking, desire is the foundation that tells me what will shift in your life and what will remain.

Little wonder the Bible was saying "as a man thinketh in his heart so is he" and child of God, God wants every child of his to do is; no matter the volume of information released unto you, the volume of revelation you are going to be carrying if your desire doesn't change, manifestation will be impossible.

And so Lazarus am aware of the fact that you are a kingdom man but you got to begin to desire like a royal, Lazarus am aware that there is something on your life but you got to change the sentence. He desired to be fed with the crumbs from the rich man's table, Lazarus helped by God he reminds me clearly of the woman and this was the kind of conversation she also had with Jesus and Jesus said you don't take what belongs to the children and you give it to the dogs and the woman looks at Jesus and says sir you are correct but even the dogs eat the crumbs from the table but in this sense he was referring to her relationship with Jesus but then again in Lazarus' sense he was referring to his relationship with the rich man.

Child of God, if only in this life we have hope, we will be most miserable, until your appetite changes, your desire remains limited. You may have not understood how powerful your desire is in the matter of manifestation.

In the matter of manifestation, desire becomes the fire, desire becomes the passion, and desire becomes the foundation that God uses to unleash himself. There's so much God wants to do and manifest to our life but the question heaven is asking –how bad do you want it? There's so much God wants to do with your life but he is looking at your desire, it's too passive.

Child of God when you become restless, there is a level of desire that wakes up inside you. No one stays on spiritual junk meals and produces a desire of a warrior. No one feeds on junk meals of the spirit and imagines that you going to produce the desire of a warrior.

All that God is saying right now is that he is on settings of your mind. God is saying there's so much I want to make happen for you but it is amounting to your desire. Lazarus don't live below your identity mandate; Lazarus don't live below what God has ordained for you.

Some of us already have an awareness that am

supposed to be at the gate who are already at the gate but sadly enough like Lazarus he was at the gate but he was wounded. Wounded man at the gate, bleeding man at the gate, full of sores at the gate, child of God, this is the devil.

The devil does not mind, remain at the gate but stay at the gate wounded, carry the microphone in your hands be singing and preaching but let me make sure you are still bleeding, announce to everyone that you are born again but I must make sure that I live you with some sores.

The mandate of manifestation in the kingdom is not a mandate of take care of your house, it's a mandate of take care of your nature, it's a mandate of take care of your city, it's a mandate of take care of your environment. A man who is wounded at the gate will spend more time nursing his wounds than protecting his territory.

The Bible says the son of righteousness shall rise with healing in its wings. Somebody say I leave my wounds behind, any wound that you came with is washed away.

No matter what you hear, the wound can distract you, no matter what you hear you will go out as your amen will sound let there be healing for your wounds. I want you to declare that I will not be wounded at the gate.

One of the son of the prophets when they told the man of God let us go and make a bigger house where we will stay with you, as one was working, as one was putting the effort a wound came and the axe head dislocated from the handle, thank God he recognized it, thank God he knew. There is a generation wounded but have no idea. Immediately their axe head fell off, they wanted to package the situation.

They still carried the wood because no one must know that we no longer have an axe head. Even though the axe head had fallen off we must not disclose there is no axe head. We must not let everybody know that there is no axe head, this is why the Lord today must see my wound, touch my wound, heal my wound.

And I kept wondering, what if he did not cry out, he would have been using a wood against a wood. And some of us it's a situation we are using a wood against a wood given to your generation what they already have, handing over to a generation what they already need because some were wounded and they lost their cartilage.

Child of God, do you realize that this man we are talking about would have had more but his desire was tied to a man. The scripture says about Lazarus that after all said and done he died, the rich man did not die before him, the rich man represented a system that had no regard for anything called kingdom that is why he abandoned Lazarus, the rich man represented a wicked system that would do anything to delete God from anything that has to do with life. Well guess what Lazarus died wickedness was still alive.

We will not let our prayer and passion die, there is yet another kingdom because Jesus says I will build my church and the gates of hell will not prevail. Whenever the church is being built, the gates of hell start fighting because he said the gates of hell will not prevail once the building starts.

And this is you replying the gates of hell just in case you are wondering are we coming up or are we going down, look at our fight. Don't look at how many members came to church, look at the extent of your fight, the extent of your fight points to your capacity.

Rich man you have no idea, am at the gate to send you out of your house because the earth is the

Lord's and the fullness thereof. Lift up your right hand, declare say right now I announce I will not die in the face of negativity, nothing will choke my faith, nothing will choke my fire, nothing will choke my grace. If you understand it say a loud Amen. The Bible says the kingdoms of this world as the angels creed, they have become the kingdom of our God. And the man Moses got to Egypt and one of the signs, he threw his rod on the ground and became a snake and the Egyptian magicians threw their own rods on the ground and they also became snakes, you know where the kingdom begins to work is the capacity of what I carry to swallow negativity. The Bible says and the rod which is the snake of Moses opened its mouth began to swallow.

# Chapter One

# DEVELOPING OUR MINDSET

Do we mentally agree with God; do we have the mind of Christ when it comes to understanding who he has made us to be?

Child of God, do you know who you are and why you're here on earth? You're the apple of God's eye. He made us in His likeness, in His own image to represent Him here on earth. In this chapter, we will be looking at the world's system and the godly system, developing our mindset, why we need to speak like kings and queens, and the main reason why we're here on earth.

We have the world's system and the godly system and what happens is if we are not guarded, the world's system talks us out of our godly nature. So you have to fight hard as a person of faith to walk in and manifest what God says.

Why? Because there are so many beliefs in this world

that the average person not educated about the system, can be talked out of their mind and convinced into another mind, contrary to the mind of God.

For instance, when we are born, we grow up in different cultures, different upbringings, and different teachings. We might all be Christians but we are taught differently. We might have been brought up through a religious system whereby what we have been taught about God varies. Things such as, He is our father yes but if we sin, we have to burn in hell, for example, kind of scary to think of it this way.

Others gave us this kind of picture of God but we have to be re-introduced to the truth of who our Father is. It's going to be a mindset adjustment or a process. It is not something that can just happen overnight because it took a process for the old mindset to be developed.

If we want to develop that mindset, we have to understand the different settings of kingdoms. When God was developing this world, He created different types of kingdoms and gave them different leaders. In the animal kingdom, we know that the lion is the king of the jungle, in the air it is the eagle that rules; even the Bible says that he will give us wings to fly high like an eagle (Isaiah 40:31). And there is the water kingdom where the whale is the king of the waters.

We have different kingdoms but the greatest thing is He gave us the earth. He says the heavens are His but the earth he has given unto man (Psalm 115:16). He has called us to dominate so we are here to dominate. Even though we have all these different kingdoms, they all fall under our authority because they are all on earth.

The Bible describes Satan as the prince of the earth so he has no authority over the earth and the greatest privilege is that we as humans have the authority as the legal entity. Even God can't perform on earth without a man. He needs a body. That is why every time He used to talk, He would say, "the Son of Man" (Luke 19:10; Matthew 18:11) because He wanted to relate with the people that He is like Him. He never said "the Son of God" but "the Son of Man" because he was relating with us. We are born of flesh.

So man is here to dominate and we are the legal entity to represent all on earth. That's why the Jews still believe the Messiah is coming. They think He is just going to drop from heaven but God has a system of how He works.

We humans are the legal entity, He needs a body and He needs a person. That's why He made us in His likeness, in His own image to represent Him here on earth. When we are walking, we are not just walking as nobody but we are carrying the Holy Spirit.

The Holy Spirit is in us causing us to manifest, to show the world how to rule and to reign as children of God.

Think about a lion, when it is born, it isn't taught how to roar. Roaring is natural for a lion. It's in their nature. It is the nature of an eagle to lead in the air just like it's the nature of the whale to lead underwater. So what am I saying? This is naturally engrained in them. With God, these things are naturally implanted in us as well.

Leadership is naturally wired into us that's why when a person is oppressed, they always fight it. Why? Because something in them says: "you are created to dominate not to be dominated". It is in our DNA. It's natural as a lion is the king of the jungle. It's natural for us to be kings and priests unto our God. The issue is that systems have talked people out of their minds because the word of God says, let this mind be in you that was also in Jesus Christ who being in the form of God thought it not proper to be equal with God (Philippians 2:5-6).

What's that to be equal in perception, in mindset, or in mentality? This is the power of what we have but systems have communicated something differently for so long. An example of this is seen when on the first day of school, students have to do an assessment to see if they can read and write and there are many people who can't do any of these.

I am not against the laws but when these systems talk you out of your mind, you can have a problem for the rest of your life with something you heard in third grade.

Mindset is so powerful because we have been taught for such a long time that we belong to a certain class. Back in those days, when we were in school, the practice was to grade persons based on whether or not they were clever and as such many persons grew up believing that they were a second class citizen as a result of erroneous practices but we need to change our mindset and believe we are kingdom citizens.

God himself lives inside of us. The God inside of us is the Creator of heaven and earth and all that is in them. When we develop such a mindset, we remove anything called limitations and we begin to see everything as possible.

In Joshua 10:12-13(NKJV), we read, [12] Then Joshua spoke to the LORD in the day when the LORD delivered up the Amorites before the children of Israel, and he said in the sight of Israel:

"Sun, stand still over Gibeon;
And Moon, in the Valley of Aijalon."
[13] So the sun stood still, And the moon stopped,
Till the people had revenge Upon their enemies.

So the sun stood still in the midst of heaven, and did not hasten to go *down* for about a whole day.

By the time you command the moon, you can command every kind of interactive thing to also stand still. How powerful that the stars and everything aligned in obedience to the voice of one person! Why? Because Joshua knew who he had inside of him. When he was saying "moon I command you to stand still" he wasn't speaking of his own authority. But in the name of the Lord.

When Jesus came, he said in **Matthew 18:18 (NKJV)** [18] "Assuredly, I say to you, whatever you bind on earth will be bound in heaven, and whatever you loose on earth will be loosed in heaven.

That is the kind of power that should be so common to us that we can bind demons and their corresponding works. You can declare today, "I bind failure; I have had enough of it and am binding it. I command you to go. And I open doors to success!"

Joshua was like any of us and we are even better positioned because Jesus came and opened our minds and eyes to what the kingdom of God is all about.
He said the kingdom of God is inside of you. That meant the Holy Ghost—the power—His breath is in us.

What I am hinting at is that we are different. We are all uniquely designed with God's DNA for God's unique assignment. This is why the Spirit of God is in you; you have been designed and created for something authentically unique.

Now one of the challenges is, as you begin to progress, life wants to program you to cultures. The actual battle that we are facing now is a school of thought. Institutions have different schools of thought. I for example I have a biblical world view. As I am writing this book, I am great like you that's reading it; I also have my biblical view. So what happened is my school of thought of life is based on the word of God. It is important for you to understand what schools of thought are hinting at you and what schools of thought God created for you.

How are we supposed to rule because restricting

each other as royals is not enough, what else can we do? How can we serve each other and how can we walk as kings and queens? The bible says in **1 Peter 2:9 (NKJV)** But you *are* a chosen generation, a royal priesthood, a holy nation, His own special people, that you may proclaim the praises of Him who called you out of darkness into His marvelous light;

In essence what does that mean or what does it look like? With our initiation into royalty, we want to dress like kings, think like kings and queens, and we even want to be able to visit actual palaces because exposure of this kind allows for the things on this earth to teach us the things of heaven. Even Jesus gave examples about kings and how when a king calls for a party, people should dress appropriately (Matthew 22: 8-13).

He always gave examples, not for any other place but earth. If he spoke in parables it was about our daily things so we are coming back to those basics. How are we to reign? How are we supposed to function? When God said go and dominate, what did that actually mean?

What is at stake here is that you now have to learn how to let the old go. This will mean gaining access to resources, books, etc. that will talk to you about having a royal mindset and of your identity in God because we are the new royals. Joshua 1:8 says if you meditate on the words of God day and night, you will get success. And this is regardless of who you are, where you come from, or your skin color.

Meditate on the word of God and you will have success. As you begin to deal with the principles of the word of God from a biblical world view you will realize they work for everyone. So as you allow the word of God to dwell in you and as you walk from the old ways to the new ways, you will begin to experience the newness of God.

Royal civility will cause you to walk into the newness of life and one of the greatest things about it, is that, it can start from here today and right now because you have to "let this mind be in you" (Philippians 2:5). You have to remove some blockages in your thinking so that your mindset can be renewed.

The mind of Christ is the mind of reigning; it's a mind of administering, and influencing. Everywhere Jesus went, He was so impactful that whenever He went off to a quiet place they missed him—some went as far as following him day and night. They were hungry for Him. Why? Because everywhere He went, He was an influence there for the kingdom of God and He passed it on to us. He said greater things shall you do than I have done (John 14:2). He was manifesting the kingdom of God everywhere He went and now it's our turn to do the same.

God is now counting on us to dominate (Genesis 1:26). Dominating means ruling. How do you rule your community, world, and church? Are you manifesting the kingdom of God or are you reacting like everyone else?

In Matthew 14:15-20, an account is given of when the disciples came to Jesus, and told Him to send the multitudes away since they had no means to feed them. Instead of agreeing with the disciples, Jesus told them to bring what was considered to be little and in turn multiplied it to be more than enough for the people to eat. Jesus was the solution!

When we go to places, we too should be the solution, light, and preservation. When we go into places that are bound, we should be the ones to speak the word of God and see people be set free. The kingdom isn't about flesh and blood it's about the power of the Holy Ghost. Where ever we walk we carry the DNA of God. We speak and things happen. At your command angels are waiting for the command of the children of God to start doing whatever needs to be done (Psalm 103:20).

Like I stated prior, dominating means to rule. Jesus ruled so much that He walked on water (Matthew 14:25). He defied the laws of science. That's what being a royal is about. We defy what the world says. We demonstrate what the kingdom of God is.

In the Old Testament (2 Kings 6:1-7), when the axe fell into the water, what did the prophet Elisha do? The axe was meant to sink but he caused it to float. In 2 Kings 2:19-22, when the water was all salty and they couldn't find any water to drink, what did the prophet do? He gave a solution that made the water drinkable because he had the DNA of God in him.

In your life as well He can change things; He can defy science. You can command a fish to bring that money that will pay off the debt like Jesus told Peter (Matthew 17:24-27). Jesus even cursed a tree that had no fruit in the moment He was hungry causing it to wither up (Matthew 21:18-22). That's how we dominate and rule. In fact, the next time you walk into a place and things are a mess, speak order to things for them to function as God wants them to function.

The bible says it's "not by might nor by power, but by My Spirit" (Zechariah 4:6). The most important person in the world is the Holy Spirit because He is the One who leads us by wisdom. One can have all the intellectual knowledge on earth but one word from God changes the whole thing.

There is no reason for you to be left helpless or

stranded after coming into contact with the words written in this book. You are a fellow royal and we want you to begin functioning in your power and authority. God lives inside of you. You are somebody. God never created junk, no matter what your skin color is or the type of hair you have, we are all somebody that is what we believe in. Nobody is a nobody. We respect each other as royals because we are children of God. We come from a sovereign King—the King of kings, Lord of lords, the Lion of Judah, He owns the heavens and earth.

The bible says God made man a little lower than the angels (Psalm 8:5) not lower than the animals. And for those people, who believe in the concept of mankind being developed from apes, don't be mistaken with that type of mindset. God breathed His very own breath into you. You are the legal entity to rule and reign. You represent heaven on earth. That's why we say that everywhere you are, you bring solutions and answers.

Wherever Jesus went, He brought answers. He brought so many answers that on one occasion people took drastic steps of removing the roof just to gain access to Him (Luke 5:17-20) for someone to be healed. Can you see yourself being in a place like Jesus, that people find their way to you for help? I encourage you to develop this sort of royal mindset.

God is counting on you and angels are all deployed for you. It will be such a shame when we go back to heaven and God says, "I gave you all this power, what did you give? How did you impact the world? How did you manifest?" And your response is, "I didn't know I had all this power". We cannot afford to overlook Gods original purpose of why we are here on earth.

What you need to do is this, you have to begin to imagine in your mind what the bible says is true about you. When you read the scriptures get it in your mind that you are living like that. Get a picture of you doing what it says is possible. Get that into your imagination and let your actions be fueled by God's word.

So you take such scriptures and start putting them into your imagination. Imagine you are doing all that the Bible says, that's how you move into this reign age.

## Be Proactive

As you walk in life there has to be a proactive side. You have to push through for what you going to have now. Make faith proactive today!
Every day we wake up our faith is waiting for us to move.

QUOTE: "GOD Made Man in His Image And In His Light." (Genesis 1:27)

What you see is all you allow GOD to see. What you see as big GOD can see as small. What you look at is what GOD sees.

Look beyond where you are today. Move in realms that you never thought possible. Step out because GOD has given you the measure of faith. How you measure it out, is the way it is measured back.

QUOTE: "Where Any Two Touch and Agree It Shall Be Done." (Matthew 18:19)

GOD has more than anything we can imagine. Stop limiting GOD to your limited imagination and ask GOD to give you HIS imagination.

My life is living proof; it is not your job to intellectually understand GOD. It is your job to walk it out by faith every single day.

QUOTE: "Life and Death Are In the Power of the Tongue, and They That Love It Will Eat the Fruit Therein." (Proverbs 18:21)

Nothing in the world can stop what GOD has prepared for you.

QUOTE: "Now Faith Is!" (Hebrews 11:1)

Believe in the word of God now; it is not tomorrow it is now if you believe!

QUOTE: "All Things Are Possible." (Matthew 19:26)

If you believe then it is possible. Get to the next level in your mentality. Nothing in this world can stop you because GOD has given you His mind.

GOD gave every man the measure of faith. With the measure of faith, you move forward; you have to drive forward.

When you are talking faith your life needs to match it. GOD is directing our steps. Picture where you lack and see it through the mind of GOD.

QUOTE: "Let This Mind Be In You Which Was Also In Christ Jesus." (Philippians 2:5)
You are walking by faith right now! The battle is for your imagination!

# Chapter Two

## ROYAL CIVILITY

As I stated in chapter one, we have the world's system and God's system. If we are not guarded, the world's system talks us out of our God nature. You have to fight hard as a person of faith because there are so many different thought systems and beliefs in the world, that the average person is talked out of their mind. When that happens the mind goes contrary to the mind of God.

We are different—uniquely designed with God's DNA for something great. It is important to know what schools of thought may be hindering you and what schools of thought God proposed for you.

In the schools of thought, people are programmed to be told that they are smart. But people don't learn that way. We have let them minimize the Biblical world view. We are the new royals and everyone should be treated with civility.

The mind of Christ is the mind of administering—it is a mind of reigning!

# 2.1 What is Royal Civility?

The next thing we will look at is, what is civility? What is the culture in royal civility? We are always talking about the culture of royal civility. What is this culture and what is your understanding of it?

People hear much about the kingdom but it is not explained. To have a kingdom, there should be a king. People need to know who the king is. If someone has a bad father it is a wrong image of who God the Father is. People need to know the goodness of the Father and the goodness of the King.

Royal civility is creating an actual biblical view of the culture of the King and His kingdom. So royal civility begins on ground level and says we are the new royals. Why? Because we are created in the image of God (Genesis 1:26).

If you are made in the image of God, who are you then? For a long time, we have degraded this opportunity. It is a free opportunity and it is an opportunity that is everlasting.

It is a powerful thing when we come into the understanding that we are co-heirs of Christ Jesus (Romans 8:17). And that we are seated in a heavenly place far above principalities and rulers (Ephesians 1:20). That is the amount of power God has given us—to be seated with Christ Jesus, the only begotten Son of God and we are also His children.

The Bible says that "whatever is born of God, overcomes the world" (1 John 5:4). So our number one goal for us to enter this culture of civility is for us to believe. We are born with this gift but we must believe first. When we get entangled with the systems of this world, we can lose sight that we belong to the royal culture.

We have access to the same mind as God. Royal civility brings royalty to where it can be done in everyone's life. You have to see this in heavenly places. What does that look like in real-time today on the ground level? It looks like you having the mind of God in your world today.

It's you believing and looking through the eyes of God. And while writing, I heard it in my spirit a voice saying "give yourself permission to be a royal"! I invite you to give yourself that permission to belong in this world.

Many times we have been beaten down, defeated, and nothing about us seems to portray that we are royals but today we want to encourage people to listen and to give themselves a chance by believing they are co-heirs with Him.

Jesus never had a mindset of limitation. Everything around Him was possible. Scripture records one occasion when Jesus was called to heal a child and upon His arrival He told them the little child was just sleeping. Those present laughed because they didn't have His mindset of possibility. Jesus spoke to the child and said "Talitha, cumi" which is translated, "Little girl, I say to you, arise." At His words immediately the girl arose and walked (Mark 5:35-42).

When Jesus resurrected the dead, it didn't end with His time on earth. There are countless instances of people who have exercised their faith and resurrected persons from the dead. And it can happen through you too, if you give yourself a chance and believe that power also resides in you. If we have the mindset that we are reigning with him, He is with us, and that He is helping us, then miracles can also be worked through us.

It is not because we are so strong or we are so religious but it is all about permitting yourself to believe in the word of God. If you look at the colonial systems of the world, when they came in, they didn't come in sitting on thrones.

They came in and created a culture of thinking. So they are capturing the actual royal seat in people's minds. There is a seed of royalty in everyone's mind. Who you allow to be seated on your throne (in the mind) would rule the throne in your mind. The royal law is the law that governs the world.

There is a difference between the rules and the laws. Rules are always changing. Laws don't change. God has given us a royal law, according to James 2:8, If you really fulfill the royal law according to Scripture, "You shall love your neighbor as yourself," you do well. So that's a law; if I treat people well, I will be treated well. If I treat people badly, I will be treated badly as well because of the law.

Royal civility is helping to create the culture of God but the culture of God has to be seated on your throne (in the mind). Whatever you let in stays in.

With royal civility, we treat each other as royals because we are valuable. God didn't create junkies. We are all valued as belonging to the God class. The King of kings who reigns in power, in authority is our Father and therefore we respect everybody. We believe that everybody is on earth for a reason, for a purpose and we fulfill those reasons and purposes by leading with our gifts. If God has given you a gift and you are leading in it, He appreciates you and we acknowledge you. We are behind you all the way because God is with you as well.

The kingdom and its kings have to function not just religiously. It is one thing to walk around and quote "I am a king". But how? If you are, where is the evidence of your rulership?

Every monarchy in the world teaches their children the customs and protocols of royalty. Guess what? We too have concepts but we have not been taught the how. Royal civility is where everyone can be a king because this kingdom is different from other kingdoms.

The tradition has been for earthly kingdoms do train their very own seed; whilst we on the other hand have been taught about our Father God and His kingdom but have not been trained. We have seen and learned much but yet we don't know how to manifest the kingdom of God.

The kingdom is the actual culture of heaven. "In this manner, therefore, pray: Our Father in heaven, hallowed be Your name. Your kingdom come. Your will be done on earth as it is in heaven" (Matthew 6: 9; 10). The kingdom is about the bringing of the culture of heaven to earth. As I say this, there are already concepts of this in people's minds because everything being stated here, we have heard it before. But the question at hand is this, "what does that look like in real-time?"

Well, it looks like the idea God has given me. The kingdom is not about religions; it is about the king's rulership. The kingdom we're talking about was described by Jesus in Luke 17:20-21: "Now when He was asked by the Pharisees when the kingdom of God would come, He answered them and said, "The kingdom of God does not come with observation; nor will they say, ⁰'See here!' or 'See there!' For indeed, the kingdom of God is ⁾within you,".

At Royal civility, we will teach you how to get those concepts and incorporate them into real life. We will help you find your royal identity. You may have questions, "Am I a royal?" or "What am I called to do?" We can help you put on a mindset to understand what it is and then who you are.

We are privileged to have HRH Clyde Rivers who is a true royal and a leading voice around the world. That's a throne that God has given him to occupy. How do you take your supernatural throne and make it natural and still be on the throne? The word of God is the key component.

We have to build a mindset but you have got to be specific on what your throne is and how it comes. It can come through an idea you receive now and six months later on, a heavenly idea can be made into existence. To enforce this royal mind, look at it like a seed; "as a man thinketh so is he".

At Royal civility, we are committed to helping people identify that idea and birth it in their spirit via various programs. It takes a process for you to discover yourself and coaching with HRH Clyde Rivers and Prof. Julian Businge is an excellent tool to walk out this process.

When you understand who you are and you understand it's about the kingdom, you can live by the laws of the kingdom. When you activate a law from the King, results will be seen.

"Give and it will be given to you" (Luke 6:38)—that's a law. Guess how I activate that law? By giving. When you don't understand the kingdom you defeat yourself by not observing the laws.

I know that "death and life are in the power of the tongue" (Proverbs 18:21)—that's the law. And so I chose to speak life—whatever I speak, I get. That is why the Word says, "My people are destroyed for lack of knowledge. Because you have rejected knowledge" (Hosea 4:6).

What do I have to lose if I don't walk like a royal? If someone says, "oh no that's for someone else, I don't belong there". What do they lose or what do they gain?

How to get started. Here, imagine whatever you are

going through and look at it from God's perspective and how big your problem is today in the mind of God.

# Royal Branding International

Our aim is to help personalities, businesses, and various especially African kingdoms tell their authentic story. This story will allow them to rewrite their future on a local, national, and international level.

Our current project since 2019 is working closely with HRH King Oyo Nyimba and HRH Queen mother of Tooro, Queen Best Olimi in Uganda to create unique Royal fashions and designs. This is aimed at blending tradition and modernity and create modern-day cultural wear.

With our international work with Kings like Omukama Oyo of Tooro: The World's Youngest Ruling Monarch as recorded in the Guinness Book of Records; African Queens and Princesses; Ministers and Ambassadors; celebrities and many other personalities.

Our services will give you the confidence needed to discover your royalty, re-right your life and rewrite your future. Our services are provided through consultation and mentorship with our Founders and Global Partners:

**Prof. Julian Businge:** Royal Fashions Expert, Royal Ambassador at Large Global Relations, and Business Strategist.

Prof. Patrick Businge: Founder of Greatness University, Royal Ambassador at Large Global Relations, Special Advisor to Monarchs, and World's First Rewrite Your Future Expert.

HRH. Clyde Rivers, Our Global Partner, Founder of I Change Nations and a leading global voice in the World of Peace and Civility.

We believe that we are all ROYALTY, we just have not yet walked in it. There is nothing painful than having untold royalty buried inside your soul. Your royalty is too valuable that it should not go unnoticed when you are gone. Your royalty is your legacy. Your royalty needs to be told, written about and monetised.

## How Are You Going To Do This? Here Is How.

- ✓ Royal Fashions
- ✓ Greatness Research & Publications
- ✓ Royal Tours

✓ Royal Studies
✓ Royal Civility show and Awards

# Royal Fashions

We will help create your own fashion line. This will allow you to dress in your own brand and make your own mark in casual, official, and ceremonial settings.

We will also create bespoke products to match with your brand such as watches, ties, shirts, stationery lapel pins, house hold items etc.

# Greatness Research & Publications

We believe that greatness leaves footprints. That is why we are the world's first institution dedicated to discovering, unlocking, and monetizing greatness in individuals and institutions.

Our focused and accessible research makes a difference in any areas of life. For example, we have researched the world's number one motivational speaker Les Brown; the multi-millionaire businessman Antonio T Smith Jr; and the great religious leader Archbishop Doye T Agama.

We have also helped religious institutions capture their greatness in books like 'The City of Refuge Changed Our Lives'. We have researched and documented the greatness of Tooro Kingdom in Uganda and written a Royal Biography for the World's Youngest King.

Let us help you write it, publish it, and share it with the world. We will help you discover the GREATNESS in your business and how to rebrand it.

## Royal Tours

We intend to visit kingdoms around the world. Recently in 2019, a team of 15 members travelled to the heart of Africa where the action is. Most people called it the Wakanda experience.

We visited Tooro Kingdom in Uganda and celebrated the 24th coronation of HRH King Oyo. You will experience the amazing culture and mingle with Kings, Queens, Princes, Princesses, and the locals.

Let us take you to Hakyooto events organised by our royal partners and experience African culture. There you will travel back in time and experience the bonfire: a place where knowledge was transmitted from the old to the young through songs, proverbs, and folklore.

Create unforgettable memories as you travel in the heart of Africa, we offer additional services like photograph your safari and document your story in a book if interested in sharing special memories and adventures.

## Royal Studies

Did you know that Article 30 of the UN Convention on the Rights of the Child states that children from minority or indigenous groups have the right to 'learn and use the language, customs and religion of their family, whether or not these are shared by the majority of the people in the country where they live'?

Can you imagine ministers and people in your kingdom learning about their ancient, current, and future royal history? Can you imagine clans and community groups gathered learning and celebrating their culture?

Can you imagine books, apps, documentaries, online exposure, and films about your kingdom? Can you imagine tourists coming from all over the world to study about this kingdom?

This is what we will do: we will create Royal Studies in your kingdom that will help people tell their story, walk out of wrong mentalities, leave the bad past, walk into every season of life prepared, and transition into life.

We will research about your kingdom and give you a report on how to align with the modern day changes and yet remain relevant to its clans, rebrand it, align it with the 21st century community and position it in the global royal news. We also have an added service of teaching Royal Diplomacy and protocol to the visitors from around the world or local community ready to learn.

By the end of the process, we will have had lots of fun, spent time with royals, influencers and change-makers, gone on tour with them, shared your message on the ROYAL STAGES, appear on our virtual WALL OF FAME and be in the royal news.

We at Royal Branding look forward to helping you manifest your royalty, create your best life, and live a legacy.

**How my business, innovation and initiative is helping my community and our world.**

- Every year, during the black history month, we get into schools and youth clubs and online to talk about African Royalty and its importance to us.

- Promoting cultural exchanges between Africa and Europe
- Teaching Royal Diplomacy and protocol to the visitors from around the world or local community ready to learn
- Travel to African Kingdoms

**An example of an act of business incivility and a business civility solution that am implementing**

An act of business incivility is discrimination. If an employee consistently sees promotions being given based on gender, race, age or other discriminatory factors, their drive to advance within the organization or perform to the best of their ability is negatively affected.

The solution am providing is bridging the gap through education and communication between African cultures and Europe and people to appreciate their self-worth and build confidence.

## 2.2 How To Gain The Ground And Keep The Ground You Gain?

QUOTE: "Let This Mind Be In You Which Was Also Christ Jesus" (Philippians 2:5); "As He Is, So Are We In This World" (1 John 4:17b).

Adopt a royal mentality. We need to see the manifestation.

QUOTE: "Without Faith It Is Impossible To Please Him (GOD)" (Hebrews 11:6).

This means it takes faith to please GOD. GOD gives us faith. Every person has a mustard seed of faith.

Stop looking for national currency and look for biblical currency. Biblical currency is the idea of GOD. Currency of faith will take and create what GOD wants to create.
Step your mind up to step your life up. Take GOD's idea to create.

GOD has a different logic. You are powered by GOD. Get out of the matrix and begin to create the next season.

If you are walking by faith and not by sight, it means you have already predicted the future of your life because you are powered by GOD. Understand the Biblical Principles because they work.

QUOTE: "His Word Is Incorruptible. It Never Returns Void." (Isaiah 55:11)

Everything GOD made is designed for success. Your seed is blessed because the word of GOD is an incorruptible seed.

The economy of GOD is created by faith. When you say you want to do something, faith turns it into existence.

Look at your issue through the mind of GOD. That's how you let the mind of GOD be in you.
If you are defeated, it is because of your mind. How big is your issue to GOD? Your issue is recorded as done on GOD's grid.

Think out of the box. Don't say "What in the hell are you looking at?" That's a dark perception. "Say what in the heaven are you looking at?"

Re-purpose your life right now. Create your future and stop letting your past define it. Create your vision; GOD will fund it. It must be HIS vision for if it is not "THE" vision GOD will destroy it.

Faith Can Buy Anything In The World. Kick the Game Up Today.

# Chapter Three

## BE GREAT ON PURPOSE

Control the currency in your mind. Don't let that currency be manipulated. The currency of the mind is a highway. Block the end roads to the mind. Everything you are up against now wants to devalue your currency.

The GOD that made you is the same GOD that will take care of you. The value of your currency is the same as GOD. This is because you are made in the same image of GOD.

GOD gave you dominion when he made you in HIS image. Life and Death are in the power of your tongue. Your job is to multiply on the earth. Block all the negative thoughts in your mind.

Everything you need is by faith. GOD has given you the vehicle of faith. People want you to think that things are created by means other than faith. We walk by faith and not by sight (2 Corinthians 5:7).

Quote: "Without Faith It Is Impossible To Please GOD."

What vehicle have you put your faith in? Faith moves GOD. GOD has a different logic. That's why we walk by faith and not by sight. GOD has another level of faith; HE wants you to look over the fence.

Quote: "The Thief Does Not Come Except To Steal" (John 10:10).

The opposite season is what we are living in right now. When you walk by faith, you are walking in victory.

Stop looking for other systems to create what GOD gives you uniquely. Systems do not validate GOD, GOD validates systems. Stop waiting for your system to be validated by the world. Stop waiting for validation and create validation.

When someone asks, "Where is the proof?" Tell them faith is the evidence. Create the next season. Speak it and walk in it now.

Stop asking permission for your greatness. You are already great because GOD created you. GOD never asked permission to do anything. He just created it. Whatever ideas GOD gives you is validated by heaven and nobody else's validation.

Keep having success. People follow success. Keep being successful in Christ's name and change will occur in the world. Faith builds your next season. Take small steps towards the big things GOD gives you and they will come to pass.

The victories are in Jesus. Those battles educate you of what you were but they do not know what you will be in the future.

GOD made you in HIS image. You are successful in skin already. If GOD is good, then YES you are good. That means you can function like GOD.

Quote: "Be Not Conformed To This World" (Romans 12:2).

That means do not conform to this way of thinking but be transformed by the renewal of your mind. You are not bad because people think you are bad. You are just operating in the wrong system. You are operating in the system where you think the world has more power than GOD. The world does not have more power than GOD

Quote: "The Earth Is The Lord's And All Its Fullness, The World And Those Who Dwell

Therein" (Psalm 24:1).

That means you have got to look to the right source, not the people. People will twist your mind.

GOD is the King of kings. If GOD made you in HIS image, then you are king. GOD spoke you into existence

Quote: "I Set Before You Life And Death, Blessing And Cursing; He Said Choose Life" (Deuteronomy 30:19).

When you find the assignment of GOD in your life. It cannot be stopped.

Quote: "Seek First The Kingdom Of GOD and HIS Righteousness And All These Things Will Be Added" (Matthew 6:33).

When you seek the kingdom first, everything else will be added. It's the intellect of the world that talks people out of the system of GOD.

# You Are A Seed

Oh yes, you are a seed. Don't get stuck looking at how small the seed is but how big the tree will be. You have to let the seed grow; GOD wants you to grow.

Water your seed with the words of your mouth. How do you water seed? How do you water the promises of God? Make declarations of what GOD says you are. If God says we are; WE ARE!

Stop allowing "doubting Thomas" to make you think you are not great. You are a seed that is growing. There is greatness within everyone. You have to water the seed. GOD's word is an incorruptible seed.

Quote: "GOD Gave Man Dominion" (Genesis 1:26).

We are powered by GOD. We are powered by heaven. GOD woke you up this morning.

Faith is not quarantined. It is a walk with GOD not a walk with religion. When you walk with GOD, He never said it would be easy.

Quote: "In The World You Will Have Tribulation;

But Be Of Good Cheer, I Have Overcome The World" (John 6:33).

God has said, "I am with you always, even to the end of the age" (Matthew 28:20).

Sometimes we fail to be thankful for what God has given us. Know what you do not have but be thankful for what God has given you. These things that GOD gives you, the world can't take them away.

Stop and look at what God has given you. It may not be everything you want but without GOD you would not be alive today.

# Ready To Design Your Life

In this section, we are going to talk about the next level. The next level you are going to walk in will be absolute greatness and you are the architect—you will be the creator.

Have a new way of thinking. Your old mentality must change. We are going to design a new way of thinking in our minds. By Jesus' stripes we were healed and we are walking in the divine favour of God today.

In this day and hour, we have to control our thinking. We have to create in our mind what is taking place. In our days, life and death are in the power in our tongue and we are creating. Never spend a lot of time with negativity coming out of your mouth.

So how do we do this? We have to build a new pathway in our mind. We have to create a new pathway in our minds to think on different things. You have to create a new knowledge based on the information of God. You have to create a new pathway for a new kind of thinking for your life. You have to forget the negativity that was thrown your way. Why? We are stepping into another season and God is for us so who can be against us?

I want to encourage you today, forget the wrong stuff. We are in a day where so much information is coming at us and that information wants to turn us away from what God has said. Your God is greater than anything else in the world. God will remain true to His word. He will be with us forever and ever and His word will never return void.

What does that mean? It means that when God has spoken something, it has to come to pass because the word of God is an incorruptible seed. You have to get out of the negative grip that wants to hold you. Create new ways of thinking and new pathways of dialogue.

The Bible says, life and death are in the power of your tongue (Proverbs 18:21), you can no longer settle for eating the fruit of negativity and that's why I've said that you have to forget all the crazy reports so they do not take hold in your life again. You were designed by God for something great. Your existence in this world means that God doesn't have any spare parts in this game and He put you here by divine design to do something the world has never seen. You are called to be an original so don't end up with your life being a copy.

Some people live lives they regret. You have been put on earth to do something great and if you are still here, there is time. There is time for you to move in, step in and do things on another level.

God is your Source. Your source is not what you think but God is; and you are designed for something that only your Source can provide. He will give you the mind, the strength, the energy etc. Believe that your presence here is for you to do something that the world has never seen. You are not here by accident; you have value.

You are so valuable that God made one of you and put His design in you. He made you unique and brought you to earth for a unique purpose and a unique                                    call.
God made no mistake when He put you in this period. He made no mistake with anything that He has done in your life. He will take part in everything that happens to you as long as you allow the process to                  take                  place.
So you are not spare parts but you are here for a main purpose and made in the image of God.

## The Power that is in the Word of God

God's word is that makes you valid. God's word is a component that makes us relevant; it's the component that makes all things work. The word of God can never return void. When faced with a situation or a circumstance, you have the power of the word of God to help bring about a change. The Bible speaks of "casting down arguments and every high thing that exalts itself against the knowledge of God…" (2 Corinthians 10:5).

The Word of God also says, "call those things which do not exist as though they did" (Romans 4:17). If you have a mountain before you, a challenge or struggle, you have to call those things that be not as though they are. That means you are looking on the other side of the mountain.

Whatever the challenge is, your vocabulary can change it just because you're made in the image of God. It will create the next season of life beyond the mountain. This is why we are walking in divine health today, we are walking in the supernatural, and we are walking in victory and the blessings of God today. I don't care what it looks like today, I challenge you to begin calling those things that be not as though they are.

The issue with most people today is that they look at the mountain and they speak and build the mountain stronger. They make the mountain bigger by their vocabulary which is wrong. You have to speak to the mountain to move.

You have to declare, "I am successful in business, I am winning at everything, I walk in divine wealth, I am powered by God, I have the mind of Christ, the victories overtake me today, favor, economies, resources, joy and peace come to me today, I am highly favoured by God, and everything I touch prospers!" This type of language has to become part of your vocabulary.

You have to create a royal vocabulary. Begin to speak like royalty, begin to speak like God, begin to call those things that be not as though they are, begin to speak to the mountain and see your victory.

You have to understand that the Bible calls us kings and priests under God and you have to capture the mentality of royalty. The mentality of royalty is when a king speaks, it becomes a law. Well, God made you in his image and you were created to dominate.

How do you dominate? The words of your mouth are the tools that put you over or bring you under. That is what it is. You have to speak to the mountain so that you create a high way over it.

Recognise that sometimes when you begin a journey, you build the blocks by faith. Have the mindset to build the institution because other people haven't seen it before. Since no one has seen it, you have to create it. This is how you win. Talk about what it takes to win, you build the winning picture in your mind and then you talk the picture into existence.

As a man thinks in his heart so he is (Proverbs 23:7). What you think of in your heart, you have to create that, you have to speak that and have to paint that picture. You have to make sure other people see it. The word of God says, where there is no vision, the people perish (Proverbs 29:18).

Let me help you understand this; the vision is what is in you. You have to paint the picture so that other people see it. HRH Clyde Rivers gives an example of when he started his business, **iChange Nations** and no one could see the value. It took him two to three years to paint a picture of what the culture of honor was.

So he is going to help you build now. What you are building, start to paint the picture now because what is in your head isn't in other people's minds. How did **iChange Nations** come to life? It came to life because of the actions he took. He did events and shared videos and photos so that people could see what the culture of honor looked like. In the beginning, he was always interrogated but what took place after two to three years was that people got the vision and now people are inquiring of him—asking how they too can be honoured!

What I am saying is as it relates to your business or whatever you are building, you have to paint a picture in the minds of the people you are going to be dealing with. If you want to change your life, you've got to paint the picture for others to see. They can't see what is in your mind and therefore you have to get a good architect to craft what they can't see in order to bring it to life. It is good to have ideas but if you don't paint those ideas for others to see, they won't understand the value. So you have to value the idea.

You take your good idea by faith and you start by asking, "okay how do I start?" Because when you get it as a revelation, it doesn't mean that people can see it too. Sometimes they can't see what you are creating. This is why in the book of Romans 4:17, we are told, "call those things which do not exist as though they did". Take the time to verbally engineer your success. Talk to people about it because what is in your head is not engineered in their thinking. The idea God gives you, others don't see it.

Begin to paint the picture in the minds of the people so they can see the success and when you paint the picture, make sure they purchase your product. They will see your vision and they can buy it. Your job right now is to narrate your success in Jesus' name. Your job is to call into existence things that have never existed.

However, remember it doesn't happen overnight. If you want success, sow your seed in the ground, let it grow and never uproot it. Let the seed die, grow, and produce fruits. Now to put this in perspective with your life, Hebrews 11:3 states, "By faith we understand that the worlds were framed by the word of God, so that the things which are seen were not made of things which are visible."

So we are reframing our world with the word of God. Can you see yourself speaking over your vision every day? If you would take the bold step to speak the word of God every day, you will be speaking into existence what God wants you to create. This is why I tell you that goodness, health, and healing—all these things and more are ours and we receive those right now. Our DNA is designed to win. Life and death being in the power of our tongue is one of the most powerful things in the world. So, are you framing your future or are you letting life frame you? Never let life frame you. You are made in the image of God and you can call those things that be not as though they are. You have the ability to step into another grade that the world hasn't seen before.

Your DNA is designed to win. God created you to win. Every fibre in your body is created to win. God created your cells to win. You have been put on this earth with a winning DNA, winning structure, and winning mindset.

## Frame Your Future

The entrance of God's word brings light (Psalm 119:130). The words of your mouth produce life and death. We have to re-engineer our thinking. Change your vocabulary. No one speaks negativity and walks out a positive life.

Re-engineer your mind. We walk by faith and not by sight. Where there is no vision people perish.

To be number one you have to think differently. You have to go in your mind where other people haven't gone yet.

When you re-engineer your thinking, you re-engineer your vocabulary.

There are people in your life who will speak words that stir up negativity; be mindful of this type of people and spend as little time as you can with them.

Focus forward, on what the vision is! Do not look at the past. Never stop moving.

The most important ears in your life are yours. Because whatever you say, your ears automatically believe.

How do you re-engineer life? When your life is at an uncomfortable level; first of all, ask for God's help, and HE will. And then with practical steps; look at where you want to go and talk about it, and then create it.

You are a seed from God; so how great is what is inside of you?

Re-engineer your thinking, re-engineer your vocabulary then reconstruct your life. Don't fear dying. I pray to God to let my cells live in my body as He has ordained. It's another way of thinking and you can do the same.

Go big with your vision. Don't play it small, don't play safe. Be great on purpose. Never let one person with small negativity control your day!

# Positive Affirmations

Positive affirmations are simply phrases that we repeat aloud. You can either repeat to yourself or you can write them in some sort of systematic way for ease of reference. What I mean by systematic is you have to set some sort of intention. For instance, why are you saying or writing what you're saying or writing? The real power of positive affirmations is in the intention behind them and how focused you can allow yourself to become on that intention.

Let's take an example: "I'm great and that's what I am." If you only say this phrase over and over and hope something will touch the depths of your subconscious without you doing very much, honestly, you'll probably be disappointed. The affirmation is like a framework for you to work in. You interact with your subconscious mind in the space you create by doing affirmations the right way.

Now, what is the right way to practice or do it?

You really tap into the power of positive affirmations by incorporating them into a daily practice. Just like anything else, you get better the more you actually do it. The more you practice, the deeper your practice can become.

Clarify your intentions, bring in your spiritual guide, utilize visualizations and allow yourself to become emotional.

In reference to the previous illustration, "I'm great and that is what I am," decide exactly why you are saying these words. What do you want to achieve by coming to believe these words? Clarify, clarify. Now, what emotions come up when you think about how great you are and the ways you've interacted with the concept over the course of your life?

Do you feel happy or unhappy? Keep on practicing it and in a short period you'll get used to it. Positive affirmations are hugely powerful. They can alter the way you think and the things you're able to manifest in your life.

# Chapter Four

# A LIFESTYLE OF DIPLOMACY

Would you like to be happier? Many of us struggle with stress on a daily basis, but changing a few of your daily habits can improve your overall well-being.

Beloved, I pray that you may prosper in all things and be in health, just as your soul prospers (3 John 1:2).

But take heed to yourselves, lest your hearts be weighed down with [a]carousing, drunkenness, and cares of this life, and that Day come on you unexpectedly (Luke 21:34).

Then He said to His disciples, "Therefore I say to you, do not worry about your life, what you will eat; nor about the body, what you will put on (Luke 12:22).

Our God wants us to take care of our body, mind,

health, etc. As royals, we need to learn how to develop a lifestyle of diplomacy. There are simple ways to make royal diplomacy applicable to your daily life, with practices such as deep breathing, living in the present, meditation, helping others, listening to conscious music, etc. Therefore, in this chapter, we will be looking at these simple ways to make royal diplomacy part of your daily life, and if properly done, how they can help us become a better person starting from today.

# Pay Attention To Your Breathing

As a human being, breathing is habitual. According to Wikipedia, breathing is the process of moving air in and out of the lungs to facilitate gas exchange with the internal environment, mostly to flush out carbon dioxide and bring in oxygen. We can see how important breathing is and how essential it is to function. We also need to be aware of the profound healing effects of breath-work.

The conscious practice of altering our breathing patterns releases blockages within the energetic body and has on calming effect on the nervous system and nourishing of our cells.

You need to pay attention to your breathing because one of the easiest ways to connect with the Higher Source is through our breath (I want you to know that, in life everything has a source. When you realize yourself beyond your body and mind, you realize your true self. When you do that, you also realize the higher self, beyond the self).

Breathing also helps in strengthening relationships. According to research, through breath-work, we can learn to understand our triggers and why we do the things we do in our relationships, which in many instances is the first step towards healing.

By using breathing in a session, you will gain deeper clarity around what's happening, and you will start to go more to the root, which really helps to facilitate the healing process for yourself and for the relationship.

It improves focus, whether we're gearing up for a job interview or we have a presentation at work. According to some experts, through mindfulness and relaxation, breathing can help us release brain fog and get into gear for the things that matter most. Experts also state that, most us can't afford to go into panic mode and deplete our performance.

We do well when we are relaxed, not when we are tight and holding the breath. By breathing deeply, you are simply bringing more awareness to the breath, which really helps with getting clear and present.

Breath is the bridge between the body and the mind. Therefore, in order to function most efficiently, we want to create a stronger connection between the body and the mind. You can think of breath-work as a tool that helps you maintain that balance, that equilibrium of body and mind.

When we're aware of our breathing, we are present to ourselves. This is awesome. This is when our mind and body are in greatest synchronicity with one another.

# Meditation

Another simple way to make royal diplomacy apply to our daily life is through meditation and breathing helps you meditate because it is one of the most fundamental aspects of meditation. Meditation presents us with one of the greatest opportunities to study the breath. When you breathe during meditation, always breathe through your nostrils, never your mouth, and consider counting the number of repetitions of the breath. When you inhale and exhale, count to one, and when you inhale and exhale again, count to two.

Meditation has become a popular practice, not only by the monks in the mountains, but of many people in cities, husbands, businessmen, wives, people with demanding jobs, and many others who are constantly affected by noise and other factors. Honestly, the power of meditation is not only limited to spiritual growth but also benefits other aspects of life, our happiness, achieving our goals, our health, overcoming illnesses, and the list goes on.

It's not only a relatively simple exercise of the mind but the power of meditation encompasses a vast number of benefits. Meditation is not only good in helping us focus our minds and helps us attain deep relaxation, but can also do wonders for our health, self-confidence, our thoughts, in finding happiness, in gaining motivation, emotional cleansing and balancing, deepening concentration, unlocking creativity, and finding inner guidance.

Note: when doing your meditation, put your

expectations aside, and don't stress out about the right way to do it. There are many ways to meditate and there is no fixed criterion for determining right meditation. What works for you is the right method for you.

Few things to avoid when you start meditation:

• Don't try to force something to happen.

• Don't try to make your mind blank or chase thoughts away.

• Don't over-analyze the meditation.

# Listen To Conscious Music

One simple way to make royal diplomacy part of your daily life is by listening to conscious music. Listening to music benefits us individually and collectively. It helps improve our physical, mental, and emotional health. The essential elements for music are harmony, melody, and rhythm. Only consciously created music incorporates all of these elements.

Music connects us and it remains a powerful way of uniting us. For instance, national anthems connect crowds at sporting events, hymns build identity in houses of worship, love songs help prospective partners bond during courtship and lullabies enable parents and children to develop secure attachments. In addition to that, music's effects on the mind is numerous.

Listening to conscious music leads to better learning, according to Johns Hopkins, who said you listen to music to stimulate your brain. In fact, scientists know that listening to music engages your brain. They can see the active areas of a person's brain light up in MRI scans.

Another benefit is that it can improve memory as well. Listening to conscious music has a positive effect on your ability to memorize. Music memory is one of the brain's functions most resistant to dementia. That's the reason some caregivers have had success using music to calm dementia patients and build trusting connections with them. Listening to music can help treat mental illness. According to research, it was found that listening to music triggers the release of several neurochemicals that play a role in brain function and mental health.

Another reason you need to listen to conscious music daily is that it can help lower anxiety. There is also evidence that shows listening to music can help calm you in situations where you might feel anxious. Music blended with nature sounds help people feel less anxious. Even those facing critical illness feel less anxiety after music therapy.

Conscious music is alive, uplifting, alert, exhilarating and flows with life whilst at the same time calms and balances the senses. It is light, joyful, non-addictive and always fresh and new. Conscious music stimulates creativity in you through the very act of listening. It carries the listener back into the silence that created—this is how important it is. It inspires and enlivens, it has integrity and authenticity, and it touches you deeply.

# Cultivate The Habit of Helping Others

Another thing I want to talk about is the power of helping others. Helping others can lead to a happier life. Let's quickly take a look at the rich people in the world. Philanthropy is just another popularized medicine for these people. If being rich did not present opportunities to help others, then wealth would be the abhorred disease. Their wealth empowers them to unleash their potential to change the world for a better and safer place to live. Therefore, we're also being encouraged to help others.

Even God said we should give. He said in Luke 6:38: Give, and it will be given to you: good measure, pressed down, shaken together, and running over will be put into your bosom. For with the same measure that you use, it will be measured back to you.

Most of the rich investments or grant programs are geared toward feeding the poor, assisting the underprivileged, mentorship, or finding the cure to some terminal illness.

Today, we see people and foundations, like the Bill & Melinda Gates Foundation, Ted Turner of Turner Broadcasting, Warren Buffet's huge donation to fight aids in Africa, and Oprah Winfrey's Angel Network being amplified for their efforts. These people are not different from you and me! They're in a position to make a change, and you too, would do the same.

# Walk Outside

Many people ask, why do we choose to walk for a healthy lifestyle? Well, we know the inner peace walking bestows upon us as we walk outside and enjoy what nature gives us. A nice walk just makes us feel better. But have you ever thought about walking as a health benefit? Going for a stroll or for an upbeat walk for the purpose of making our bodies healthier has become an international rave in exercise. Being in nature reduces stress, makes you more creative, improves your memory and may even make you a better person.

Also, it's even more beneficial to take your exercise outdoors when possible. Research has shown exercise improves sleep, increases libido and makes you feel better about your body. Exercising every day is an integral part of the equation for optimum health. And exercise is the number one stress buster, boosts your energy level, increases metabolism, aids in digestion, and lowers the risk for developing heart disease and high blood pressure.

Where possible, we should take advantage of the easiest means to make exercise an everyday part of our lives. If you belong to a gym, do make a special effort to get there—sometimes you have to give yourself the extra push but just do it! On the other hand, just leaving your home for a walk takes far less effort, saves time and creates far less air pollution.

In fact, you can even just walk out your office door at lunch time. Plus, taking a walk after eating lunch will stimulate digestion, you will enjoy some sunshine, and you will boost your energy level to get through the afternoon. And you haven't added any extra time to your daily schedule. Once you arrive home, you can relax all evening—your exercising is already done.

## Stay In the Present

It holds significance when a person can stay in the present. The purpose of life is to live meaningfully. If you allow yourself to not treasure the simple things, you fail to take advantage of the gift of life.

There will be times in your life where you find yourself rushing to get to the next thing – your job, your partner, your appointments - without any consideration or participation in the current thing, whatever that might be. It's like sticking your head out the window of a speeding car. You are unable to clearly see anything, whether it's right next to you, in front or behind.

Life is in its most perfect state when you're present in every moment. Living in the past or future, as we often do, only serves to drain your spirit. You can't change what has happened, nor can you worry about what hasn't happened yet. So instead of living in the land of "I could have, should have, would have" or "what if?"—try living in the land of "I am", because now is the only moment you can affect and enjoy. Immerse yourself wholly in the present moment and put all your attention and focus on what you are doing right now.

## Spend Time with Friends and Family

Daniel Gilbert, Harvard happiness expert, said spending time with friends and family is one of the biggest sources of happiness in our lives. Relationships are worth more than we think. Not feeling socially connected can make us feel sick and even depressed. Loneliness can even lead to heart attack, stroke, and diabetes.

History has shown that the people who lived

longest, all placed a strong emphasis on social engagement and good relationships are more important to a long life than even exercise. Your immediate loved ones and friends are key to improving your life. Share good news and respond enthusiastically when others share good news with you to improve your relationships.

# Drink a lot of Water

The last thing I will highlight is the importance of adequate water intake. I know you would like to know the benefits to drinking a lot of water. Well, the first benefit is on the brain. Brain cells that have plenty of drinking water are able to circulate fresh, oxygen-laden blood more readily. This way the brain remains fresh and alert. Even a small drop in water consumption levels can make your brain's performance level drop by as much as 20-30%.

Another benefit is that water acts as a cooling system. Your body's temperature is maintained through drinking water. The water regulates body temperature through sweat. To maintain a normal temperature of 96.6 degrees Fahrenheit on hot days, or when exercising, the body sweats. Sweat cools the body, but sweat uses up water. You must have a lot of drinking water to replenish the supply.

Nerve cells transmit messages to and from the brain. To do this, they must use electrolytes. Drinking water is an important way to maintain electrolytes at the proper level so that the nerves can do their work.

Eye and mouth protection is just another benefit of drinking lot of water. Water keeps your eyes and mouth moist. It washes dirt and dust away from your eyes. Lastly, drinking water is oiling your body's joints. Water lubricates the joints, keeping them flexible, and ensuring smooth motion.

# Chapter Five

## A ROYAL MINDSET STARTS WITH EDUCATION

The royal mindset is an example that was evidenced in the life of MAMA SARAH OBAMA who transitioned this life on March 29, 2021. She was the type of individual who had the mindset to educate people through her tireless efforts that spanned over eighty (80) years. During this time she served mankind to help them understand the importance of education.

Education helps you to mind your own goal. Mama Sarah's efforts were seen in educating orphans, especially how hard she worked to educate girls in Kenya when she was growing up, in the period where women were not allowed to receive an education.

Even during this time MAMA SARAH OBAMA still understood the importance of education. She understood that education is the gateway to open a world of learning for people and gives people the ability to have equality in life. She committed her life to bring education and empowerment to people in Kenya and around the world.

Her effort of bringing education to the world is a key component of the royal mentality. So I want to encourage everyone, if you want to make the world a better place, you must help people to adopt a royal mindset and that mindset starts with education.

# Creating and Establishing Victories!

**Power is belief! Power is in your system!**

The word of God is forever settled in heaven. It's the only thing that will never return void. The word of God is an incorruptible seed. When you have an understanding of God, you step into unprecedented victories; you walk into another dimension.

The problem is our belief system; you have to modify your belief system to line up with God.

**QUOTE:** *"Let This Mind Be In You Which Was Also In Christ Jesus, Who, Being In The Form Of God, Did Not Consider It Robbery To Be Equal With God"* (Philippians 2:5; 6).

This means we can have the mind of GOD. We can have GOD's perceptions. We can walk out of GOD's mind. GOD's mind is the unlimited mind. When you allow the unlimited mind of GOD to become your perception, then you experience change.

This also means you, like Christ Jesus, have the power to be equal with God in your mentality. People walk according to their belief systems. If you believe wrongly, you will walk out wrong things.

**QUOTE:** *"I Have Come To Give You Life And Life More Abundantly"* (John 10:10).

What happens when you let that abundant mind of God live in you? Practically, you look at your life through the abundance of God. Imagine all the debt you have; imagine it through the eyes of the One who pays all debts. If you have sickness in your body, look at the One who paid the price for your healing. Look through the eyes of the unlimited mind of God; and then you will be able to see the things He has set for your life.

**QUOTE:** *"Cast Down Arguments And Every High Thing That Exalts Itself Against The Knowledge Of GOD"* *(2 Corinthians 10:5).*

So if you have thoughts that exalt themselves above the knowledge of God, you must bring them under the knowledge of GOD.

When your thought patterns are negative, you produce negative outcomes. People cannot negate the wisdom of God. The mind of God comes from a different logic. Jesus has a different logic. The logic of God doesn't make sense to the natural mind. God's logic is faith. You have to walk by faith. Evict negativity from your belief system. Evict the wrong mentality. Command your mind to obey the mind of God.

Step into being that proactive person and challenge yourself to be proactive. Don't settle by merely saying you will wait for the day; you bring the day and decide *today*! Words in your mouth have to accomplish things first.

**QUOTE:** *"Death And Life Are In The Power Of The Tongue"* *(Proverbs 18:21).*

Speak of life if you want to produce life. Practically try faith pushups. Speak the word of God until it gets in your mind. When you hear words of life, all you need to do is receive it.

**STAY UP, WIN EVERYTHING!**

# How To Have The Race Talk

How do you have a tough conversation that involves race?

What matters is how people see each other. When emotions are high intelligence is low. Everyone's experience is all they know. Your experience is all you know.

If you devalue someone's experience you devalue them.

Come with a heart of learning when having a race conversation. When histories collide we have to listen to each other for a change.

If you don't want to hear answers, then don't ask questions. If you want to prove a point, then that is a long way to go. Within our experiences, we all have prejudgments that bias our minds.

Do not gaslight an issue. This means; "When you say black lives matter and another says all lives matter; no one implies all lives don't matter. Rather, right now it's the black man's life that is in need."

You have to be honest. If you know systems are unjust don't hide from it, acknowledge it. We have to check our hearts and thoughts.

Understand each other's histories. Come to the table and educate each other about one's history. Put down your bias. Learn to build a conversation with a dialogue.

Everyone needs to be heard and they have to be willing to listen. We need to have conversations when conversations need to be heard, not after.

# CONCLUSION

GOD is about to make His people great. GOD does not work against you. We are the HEAD and not the TAIL. We have to stretch our mentality.

GOD's size favor is unlimited. It's above what you can imagine. GOD wants us to understand how big HE is and is moving on our behalf.

GOD wants to give us his mentality, because we have the mind of Christ. Do not look for victory, you are victory. GOD is taking every limit off. He is bringing into your life the most amazing things you can imagine.

Expect the unexpected from GOD. When you have a dream, dream BIG because GOD gave it you. GOD is giving you unlimited VICTORIES.

We have been faithful over the little. GOD says you are the ruler over much. GOD is not withholding any good thing from us.

Stop using words like "I CANT". NO! Those are self-imposed CURSES. Change your mentality!

GOD put wealth in every one of us. Ask for the

wealth of GOD. Don't talk about the wealth of the wicked; that will come to you anyway.

"Wealth is not seasonal; my wealth is a lifestyle" says the spirit of GOD. It is unlimited. Don't put your actual standard based on this world.

GOD has given us a new season. All you have to do is receive it!

# ABOUT THE AUTHORS

## HRH King Amissah 1 (Sir Clyde Rivers)

Sir Clyde Rivers has been given the title of, "godfather of civility". His tireless work around the world to bring one concept to people around the globe is commendable. His conviction is that kindness and respect for all humanity is the way forward to make the world a better place.

HRH Clyde Rivers is a congressional award winner in the United States of America. In 2019, he won the Nelson Mandela International Peace Award and its accolades for his service to humanity have not gone unnoticed by the world

He has met with world leaders on every continent to help highlight the salient concept of civility for all. This is the mantra that HRH Clyde Rivers has stood by and unwaveringly upholds.

He understands the importance of 7.8 billion people in the world having the ability to bring their God given gift to the world. Civility is evident in HRH. River's life in the way he engages with friends and as he works with people from different social statuses—regardless of their financial standing he treats them with kindness and respect.

It's the civility humanitarian who loves the people they are working with and understands the importance and the power of every individual in this world that their contribution helps to make this world a better place.

# Prof. Julian Businge

Professor Julian Businge is a successful, multi-passionate entrepreneur. Known for her expertise in transforming ideas into reality; identifying development projects; along with high yielding properties that generate lucrative returns, Julian provides distinctive opportunities with exciting financial rewards.

Julian received recognition as the iChange Nations (ICN) World Civility Business Woman of the Year 2020 in Great Britain. She is the Founder and CEO of Royal Civility Global Initiative, a firm that specializes in helping persons discover, develop, and celebrate their true identity through the Word of God. In 2020, Julian also became a world Civility Ambassador. And is the United Nations representative for the Peace Society of Kenya.

Julian offers forums allowing for in-depth conversations on all things pertaining to divine royalty, property, and business.

# Our Current Publications

- ✓ Breakthrough Declarations Of A Praying Wife
- ✓ Breakthrough Declarations To Receive Money
- ✓ Children Bible Stories
- ✓ Increase Your Cash Flow
- ✓ The Culture Of Royal Civility
- ✓ Yega Orutooro
- ✓ Royal Civility Magazines

# Sow this Book into Someone's Life

Don't let the impact of this book end with you

www.julianbusinge.com

Contact us: royal@julianbusinge.com

Or connect on social media:

Facebook Page: royal civility

Thank you and looking forward to celebrating with you, great testimonies, Amen.